IF I KNEW I WAS GOING TO HAVE THREE BOYS, I WOULD HAVE PAID MORE ATTENTION IN PE

Amber McClain Shaw

Velvet Fig, Inc.
Los Gatos, California

IF I KNEW I WAS GOING TO HAVE THREE BOYS,
I WOULD HAVE PAID MORE ATTENTION IN PE

Copyright © 2021 by Amber McClain Shaw.

All rights reserved. No part of this publication may be reproduced, distributed or transmitted in any form or by any means, including photocopying, recording, or other electronic or mechanical methods, without the prior written permission of the publisher, except in the case of brief quotations embodied in critical reviews and certain other non-commercial uses permitted by copyright law. For permission requests, write to the author, at: amberdesign999@gmail.com.

Author Name
Amber McClain Shaw

Published by Velvet Fig, Inc.

Contact Information
Amber McClain Shaw/Velvet Fig, Inc.
15700 Winchester Blvd
Los Gatos, CA 95030

If I Knew I Was Going to Have Three Boys,
I Would Have Paid More Attention in PE / Amber McClain Shaw. —1st ed.

ISBN 979-8-9850942-0-6

IF I KNEW I WAS GOING TO HAVE THREE BOYS,
I WOULD HAVE PAID MORE ATTENTION IN PE

*To my husband,
my partner in parenting
and other joys and challenges of life.*

*To my sons, Bennett, Kieran and Ronan,
who provided both the material and the
inspiration to write these stories.*

*To Kieran,
for encouraging me,
as you came out of general
anesthesia after surgery,
to keep writing.*

IF I KNEW I WAS GOING TO HAVE THREE BOYS,
I WOULD HAVE PAID MORE ATTENTION IN PE

Introduction

When my sons were ages seven, nine and ten, it was becoming clear that my background as the oldest of three girls had not equipped me at all for the task at hand.

Things were really different in the family I was raising.

I should have paid more attention in PE.

This is the first of three volumes. The stories are true, but some details have been changed to protect the somewhat innocent. I recommend reading these volumes chronologically, but you will find a poignant or humorous story no matter which volume you pick up.

Dinner Date

Bennett, age 10
Kieran, age 9
Ronan, age 7

I went on a date with one of the most handsome, fun people I know. My son Ronan.

He got to pick the restaurant. We went to a local high-end café, complete with white tablecloths, candlelight, soft jazzy music, and other people on dates.

Ronan was the shortest guy in the whole restaurant, but he was certainly one of the most well-behaved dates. He talked about interesting things. He noted that nice restaurants should have a fish tank. He was convinced this one did, but we couldn't see it. He had good manners. He used his salad fork to share a bite of my salad. He made a ukulele with the Wikki Stix, and we took turns playing air-ukulele to the theme from Pink Panther playing softly in the restaurant.

He did not talk loudly on his cell phone as one of our fellow diners did. As he tucked into his half order of baby back ribs, I stupidly asked, "Are those ribs better than the ones I make?"

Ronan answered, "Mom, these ribs are really good. Period." Wow, did he learn that diplomacy from his father?

The man on the cell phone, sitting near us, ordered a diet Coke and loudly slurped on the straw. Ronan didn't even think of ordering a soda, instead he sipped ice water. He did have a momentary lapse and tried to eat an ice cube off the table without using his hands. After all, he was seven years old.

During dinner, we talked and Ronan only had eyes for me. Unlike one of the other diners on a date, he wasn't trying to flirt with the waitress. As we ate and others realized he wasn't going to throw food around or start screaming, they gave us what I like to call the "cute look." Aware of the attention, Ronan did make a bit of a show with the warm towel brought to him after finishing off the ribs. He stood up, opened the large towel, and all of a sudden, slapped it on his face and head, getting himself completely wet.

He picked out a flourless chocolate cake for dessert, exactly what I would have ordered, and we shared it. When the bill came, I handed it to him.

He stared at me very wide-eyed, and said, "I have to pay?"

The Need for Speed

Bennett, age 10
Kieran, age 9
Ronan, age 7

On a trip to a lake, I was an observer to the phenomenon known to boys: the need for speed. And the corollary phenomenon: getting air.

Bennett said at one point, "I have SUCH an adrenaline rush!"

The weather was hot, and we were on a long thin lake, with a new 350-horsepower speedboat, hundreds of dollars worth of gasoline, waterskis, tubes, ropes, wakeboards, and surfboards.

We were visiting friends willing to share all this. Our friend taught the boys the two most important rules of being towed: knees bent, arms straight, and follow the boat. Oh, we had to add one more. When you fall, let go of the rope.

These friends even provided something else very exciting. The boys had the pleasure of hanging out with Travis, our friend's 17-year-old son, an extremely friendly guy with a ready smile who actually talked to them. Travis showed the boys what he could do on that wakeboard of his: get lots of speed, get lots of air, do a 360 while in the air, and then land it. My sons thought he was probably the coolest person who had ever walked the face of the earth.

This was the first time my boys had tried waterskiing. Much to my amazement, both Bennett and Kieran (Ronan wasn't there) got right up on their first try, zooming around the lake. Then my husband got right up on the skis too.

Now the pressure was on. My boys' sense of adventure inspired me to give it a try. What the heck, it was 103 degrees out, and I had to get wet anyway. I got up on my second try, and hung on for as long as I could, trying to feel the thrill they felt when they got this kind of speed. I didn't really get it. The speed scared me more than thrilled me.

Later, the boys whipped and bumped around behind the boat on a tube at high speed, the driver determined to throw them off. The boys laughed maniacally and hung on like barnacles. When they did get thrown off, they did helicopter spins, skipping across the water like stones. I did my best to suppress the momentary panic that they were hurt. That was the most adrenaline I experienced over the weekend. They surfaced, laughing and wanting more.

Then they tried wake surfing. They were fascinated by the mechanics of getting the boat set up for it, pumping water into a tank just for this purpose on one side of the boat. This created a large and steady wake that looked and acted a lot like an ocean wave, except it didn't die out and hit the beach, it just kept going, right behind the boat. Bennett and Kieran were both able to get right up on the surfboard, and surf the wave, even dropping the towrope while surfing. It was quite remarkable that they could both make it look so easy on their first try.

Then came the wakeboarding. Unbelievable, they could do that too! And they loved it.

Travis told me, "You're pretty much screwed."

And I knew he was right.

After such an active and adrenaline-filled day, they ate large amounts of bacon, left socks lying around, and didn't have to take a shower. They roasted marshmallows over the BBQ with battery-powered spinning skewers.

Can life get any better?

If I Knew I Was Going to Have Three Boys,
I Would Have Paid More Attention in PE

Sports Survival

Bennett, age 10
Kieran, age 9
Ronan, age 7

Zipping through the grocery store, I was wearing a shirt for the Nine-Year-Old All Stars Little League team. A woman came up to me and said, "Oh I've spent a lot of time at Little League games." She went on to tell me how she has three boys, and they all played baseball.

Maybe she could offer me the holy grail of surviving innumerable baseball games. I quickly asked her, "Any advice for me?"

Her advice was "Just enjoy it. If they play football, you will be sitting there for six hours at a time."

Umm, football? I hope not. I don't like football and can't understand what they are doing, dodging around on the field, anyway. I've been to only one NFL game in my life. I brought my knitting, and embarrassed my husband, which was not an easy accomplishment. I got a lot done on that knitting project, despite the rude people trying to edge by me with overfilled beers. I didn't think I'd be invited to another game, and I was fine with that.

"Yes," she explained, "I had one on varsity and one on JV. One game right after the other." I regarded her with sympathy, but she had a smile on her face. Then she told me her oldest, who was 33 years old, still played baseball and is on an All Stars team. My god, it never ends!

I took her advice to heart. Just enjoy it. I realized I better learn to become a sports fan.

Shoe Shopping, Boy Style

Bennett, age 10
Kieran, age 9
Ronan, age 7

Shoe shopping was something we had to do fairly often. The boys all wore out their shoes, if they didn't grow out of them first. I couldn't buy shoes for them without trying them on, and they had opinions about what shoes they liked and didn't like, and how they felt. To lessen the pain of taking them shopping, I usually took all three and tried to get it over with at once.

So, we shopped for shoes at a large department store nearby. We could get into the store without walking through the dreaded mall. They got to ride the escalator. It was not the cheapest place to get shoes, but it lessened the pain of shopping considerably.

It was a military style operation. Get in. Get out. It was really a bonus to get a good shoe salesperson. In fact, I found it essential. Otherwise, you might have to waste time browsing (a swear-word for boys). And then you've lost all hope of a relatively smooth shopping mission.

On one expedition in particular, we got a fabulous salesman. After ten seconds of the dreaded "browsing," the boys sat down. The salesman approached, looked at the boys and the shredded shoes on their feet, and asked what kind of shoes they were looking for. He got, in return, the stare of Boys-Who-Hate-to-Be-In-a-Store. Not getting an answer, he asked, "Should I just bring you some cool shoes?" He got a few grateful affirmative nods. In response, he smiled. He knew what he was dealing with and was up for the task.

He didn't bring velcro tennis shoes. He didn't bring skater shoes. He did not bring suede anything. What he did, was brought cool shoes. Top brand running shoes, with cool colors and cool shocks on the bottoms. He got, in return, a grateful "Yeah!" from all three boys, and me, when he asked if they were acceptable.

But then, and this was crucial, he made sure the shoes fit. Boys spend so much time on their feet, jumping and running around, that it's vital their shoes fit and don't fall off. They all got a pair of shoes they liked, that fit, without the pain of an extended shopping trip. Win, win, win! As a bonus, they each got to run a lap around the shoe department, as fast as they could, to demonstrate the speed of the briefly clean shoes.

Just when we found that great shoe salesman, Kieran outgrew children's sizes. His feet were the same size as mine! He graduated to the bigger shoes in the men's department, with the bigger price tags. I was not able to take them all shopping at once, and he was not invited to run a lap to determine how fast the shoes were.

Dirty Play

Bennett, age 10
Kieran, age 9
Ronan, age 7

We traveled to Montana for a family friend's bar mitzvah. One of the nights on the trip, we went to a big BBQ at the family's home.

The boys enjoyed a rousing game of what they called "dirt football," which basically consisted of hurling big handfuls of fine dusty Montana dirt at each other.

They have never had a better time.

One boy, usually clean and put together, came over and completely freaked his mother out by shaking his thick head of normally silky shiny brown hair, and created a cloud of dust around him, exactly like the PigPen cartoon.

His mom was wearing a white outfit, so she made a hasty retreat, and instructed all the boys to not come anywhere near the adults. Absolutely delighted with this result, the boy exclaimed, "This is SO fun!"

IF I KNEW I WAS GOING TO HAVE THREE BOYS,
I WOULD HAVE PAID MORE ATTENTION IN PE

Onions That Are Not

Bennett, age 10
Kieran, age 9
Ronan, age 7

My boys were adventurous eaters, and liked all kinds of food. On our trip to Montana, as we lazily floated down the Glacier River, my husband asked Kieran if there was any food he didn't like.

"Onions that are not caramelized," was his answer.

I love that kid.

Last Days of Summer

Bennett, age 10
Kieran, age 9
Ronan, age 7

It was the bittersweet last days of summer, my mind occupied with all I had to do before school started, and how to make this transition smooth for the boys.

We had an idyllic summer, spending most of our time in Santa Cruz. We escaped our regular school year life and lead a very child-centered, outdoor simple life. We didn't do much we didn't really want to do. We didn't attend birthday parties, we didn't meet friends for playdates unless they came to us, we didn't get in the car unless we really needed to. We didn't worry about how clean the house was, we didn't go shopping, we didn't watch any TV. We ate dinner outside almost every night, something grilled with very few dishes to clean up. The boys wore swimsuits every day and didn't have to comb their hair. We spent a lot of family time, just being together, without many distractions. We play Uno and Sorry and read books.

I wondered if it was too idyllic. Re-entry into the school year was hard on all of us after a summer like this. We all had a hard time moving straight into the rigid structure and all the expectations. The boys suggested we move to the beach, where they could be homeschooled, and continue to have lots of time to skimboard. They really weren't ready to go back.

Over Labor Day weekend, we wrapped up our summer. We spent all day at the beach, ate lunch at our favorite taquería, and spent the evening outside with good friends. My husband and I went for a walk at 11:30pm, while the boys slept. We savored the sand in our beds and slept in.

I didn't want summer to end any more than my kids. Sure, I looked forward to the routine of school. But I would miss the unstructured days and the long stretches of being together. Go back we must, to school and soccer and work and all of our various commitments.

I couldn't help but wonder how I could hold on to some things we so loved about summertime. Each one of my boys, when asked their favorite thing about summer, simply answered: being at the beach. They each loved it, for different reasons. It was a place to be with friends or play by yourself, to chat the day away or bury yourself in a book. The beach was a place to burn every ounce of energy they possessed, or simply sit and build a sandcastle. It was a place to dig a big hole. A place to see pelicans, dolphins, an otter, or the occasional gang member. A place to study tattoo art. You never know, there could be a wedding, a photo-shoot,

or a fight any given day on the beach. There could
be a teenager smoking a joint or a lone man dancing
hula. The magic of the ocean meeting the land
was somehow never boring, and melted away
any worries or stress, leaving mind and body
swept clean.

We would all miss the beach desperately. But
not enough for me to seriously consider home-
schooling these boys so they could skimboard
all day.

IF I KNEW I WAS GOING TO HAVE THREE BOYS,
I WOULD HAVE PAID MORE ATTENTION IN PE

It Never Goes Away

Bennett, age 10
Kieran, age 9
Ronan, age 7

I got a traffic ticket. Not like it was any big secret. All three of my boys were in the minivan with me when I was pulled over.

As I pulled on to the shoulder and the officer approached, the boys all sat very straight and still, not saying a word. The officer explained why he pulled me over, and then went on to inform me that I qualified for traffic school. After traffic school, he said, my ticket would then "go away."

"HA!" I said. "You see those three kids in the back? This ticket will never ever go away."

After the officer left, and we pulled back in to traffic, Bennett asked me, "Should we tell Dad about this, or not?"

After a momentary pause, I told him that we don't keep secrets like that in our family. My husband had gotten a ticket, also with the kids in the car, so he would understand.

I looked at my traffic school options. I went to traffic school once before, when I was in college. It was a very long and boring affair. The most interesting thing about it was my classmate with thick glasses who got a ticket for reading a book while driving. Things had improved since then.

My Traffic School options now included:

Comedy School

Cheap School

Fun N Cheap Comedy Traffic School

Saturday or Sunday Painless School

Pizza For You Comedians School

The Smart Choice Traffic School

I chose Fun Painless Pizza Comedy Traffic School. No children allowed, and food provided. I was eagerly awaiting it.

Picky Eating

Bennett, age 10
Kieran, age 9
Ronan, age 7

One night I didn't have time to cook, but I wanted all of us to have an enjoyable meal. And it needed to happen rather quickly. Everyone was hungry and cranky. So, with a burst of desperate creativity, I invented our first Small Bites dinner from the selection of leftovers in the refrigerator.

In the refrigerator, I had a leftover Caesar salad and some left-over vegetable quesadillas, and a couple of slices of grilled tri-tip.

I started with the salad. I found a recipe for something called Caesar Salad Soup. Following the directions, I dumped the day-old salad in a bowl. This particular salad had corn and black beans, and strips of tortilla along with the usual romaine lettuce. Then I cut up a tomato and tossed it in, and added about two cups of chicken stock. The recipe called for the mixture to sit at room temperature for an hour. Perfect. I jumped in the car and went to pick up two of the boys from soccer practice.

Lynley, a friend who was visiting, was rather disgusted at the thought of eating my concoction for dinner. I thought she would throw the mixture away while I was gone. However, when I returned, she had been distracted by Ronan, who engaged her in a game of rollerblade basketball. She didn't have a chance to sabotage the dinner.

The soup recipe then called for blending the mixture "just short of smooth" and tasting for salt and pepper. It looked a lot like vomit blended up. But I tasted it and it was pretty good! I decided to rename it gazpacho and portioned it out as shots in some small glasses. Then I cut up the leftover quesadillas and meat into little bite-sized pieces and arranged it artfully on a big white plate, and heated it all up. I added a bit of other random leftovers, and voilà, Small Bites Dinner!

Then, instead of silverware, I gave everyone a toothpick. The boys didn't like the gazpacho. However, they did love eating dinner with a toothpick. Of course, they were starving, which made almost any food, as long as it didn't look like a small glass of vomit, seem attractive. Eating with a toothpick had benefits: it slowed us all down, and we had more time between bites for conversation, even after soccer practice.

How to Save A Life

Bennett, age 10
Kieran, age 9
Ronan, age 7

Kieran came home from school today with a great story about his teacher.

She saved someone's life once, he said. Actually, she had saved two people. But the first time, she saved a kid who was choking on a hot dog.

She gave him the "Heineken maneuver."

Tree House Sleepover

Bennett, age 10
Kieran, age 9
Ronan, age 7

We were hosting a party at our house and needed someone to watch our kids. Our friends Emily and Jon offered to take them for a sleepover. With their eight and four-year-old, there were five boys in all.

The boys came home the next day raving about what a fantastic time they had. All five kids slept in the treehouse that Jon built. No one was cold, reported Bennett. Emily reported that all five were up early, 4:30am to be exact.

They recorded the exact time because they were jolted out of bed by the enthusiastic shouts of five boys playing a rousing game of soccer in the back yard in the pre-dawn moonlight.

Emily managed to return my boys with a smile on her face.

Now that is true friendship.

Multi Tasking Doesn't Work

Bennett, age 10
Kieran, age 9
Ronan, age 7

I was doing too much at once. Cleaning up dinner dishes, supervising three kids doing homework, scooping cookie-dough ice cream, thinking about conflicting soccer and football practice times, making sure everyone showered, and listening to Bennett practice a campaign speech for 5th grade rep.

And at the same time, I caught up with my husband about the day, attempted to create a school library volunteer spreadsheet, and got a head start on snacks for the week by boiling up some hard-boiled eggs.

Something had to give. It was one thing too many.

I forgot the eggs on the stove.

Ever wonder what happens if you really, really hard-boil eggs, so much that the water evaporates out of the pan? Let me tell you. They make an odd popping noise that is unidentifiable from across the house. Then they explode, sending egg and shell shrapnel all over the kitchen.

And they stink. I mean, really reek.

I threw the whole thing, pan and eggs, outside and called it a day.

A Day of Firsts

Bennett, age 10
Kieran, age 9
Ronan, age 7

It was a big day in my family. We had our first orthodontist appointment and our first football practice.

There was good news and bad news at the orthodontist. The bad news: yes, Bennett needed braces. The good news: he didn't need the braces for a few more years, until 7th grade.

Bennett then went to his first football practice. There was good news and bad news about that too. The good news (I think) is that he made the team. He reassured me that flag football was a non-contact sport. While playing this non-contact sport in PE last year, he chipped his permanent front tooth from contact with another boy. I wasn't convinced.

The bad news was that our dinner table conversation as of that night consisted of all kinds of crazy-sounding sports mumbo jumbo that I couldn't understand. It was like everyone in my house except me learned a foreign language overnight. Then the schedule came out of the backpack and the weight of the realization hit me. I was going to have to go to football games.

I thought that one NFL game would be my last football game for a good long time. I was wrong, and I didn't think I could get away with knitting during my son's game. I'd be too busy trying to figure out what was going on.

Having and raising children can push you in all sorts of unexpected and challenging ways. I wondered if this is how my brother-in-law, who played football in high school, felt as he played Barbies, listened to the High School Musical soundtrack, and painted his toenails with his two daughters.

Sock Foraging

Bennett, age 10
Kieran, age 9
Ronan, age 7

Bennett had a good excuse for running late. He claimed it took him a long time to get ready in the morning because he had to "forage for socks."

The use of the word forage gave me a chuckle. Yes, he did have to hunt, search, look, rummage around, ferret, root about and scavenge for socks.

Laundry was not one of my strong points. Three boys produced plenty of dirty clothes. I didn't enjoy it, and it was one of those jobs that is never done. I hoped that my boys were just about old enough to significantly contribute to the effort if they wanted clean, organized clothes.

Maybe if they got frustrated over having to forage for socks, they would take laundry more seriously and start to participate in it.

But no, that did not happen. They would instead discover they could wear mismatched socks. Or in desperation, my socks.

The Talk

Bennett, age 10
Kieran, age 9
Ronan, age 7

Many parents dread it. Many put it off, or simply avoid it altogether. Yes, it's the Facts of Life discussion.

My husband and I had been planning and reading and fretting and procrastinating all summer about talking to our two older boys about the subject. We really didn't know how much they knew about it all.

Up to that point, they hadn't asked many questions. Once, Bennett did ask me what sex was. He was in kindergarten, and his brothers were four and two years old. Of course, we were all in the car together, and the question came out of the blue. I remember I took a deep breath, trying to figure out how to answer. Then, after a pause, he answered his own question, "Oh, I know, it is the difference between boys and girls." He was quite satisfied with his answer, and frankly, so was I.

But I knew that I had narrowly avoided The Talk, and the subject would have to be dealt with in a much more comprehensive way. Soon, a trained educator would come in to talk with Bennett's grade, and they would start sex ed. My husband and I thought, OK, it's time, we need to give him some information before he learns about it from a stranger at school.

I got out the books, *Where Did I Come From?* and *What Is Happening to Me?* by Peter Mayle, published in 1973. As I looked through the books, I realized that they were written for kids a bit younger. However, it seemed like a good place to start, using straightforward language, illustrations, and humor to impart the basics. The facts really had not changed since 1973.

Bennett read the books first. His reaction was somewhat incredulous. "Some of this stuff is gross!" he said. To my surprise, he really didn't know much. We talked quite a bit about the section on puberty, which he was most interested in, and how things will change when as he gets older. Then he was done and wanted to go outside and throw a football around.

Kieran was next. He read the books more quickly than his brother. I suspect he skimmed over some sections. Then we sat down and went through the books and talked about them. His reaction was, "This stuff is weird." Then he wanted to go outside and throw a football around.

There was no drama, no giggling, no embarrassment (that I could tell). It was a very straightforward and basic discussion. It wasn't nearly as bad as I thought it would be.

We decided that Ronan was a bit young for the same discussion and asked that Bennett and Kieran not share all of their newfound information with him. My main concern with Ronan was that he would announce to all his friends at school exactly what he learned.

I just didn't want a phone call from another second grade parent, letting me know what a good job I did of explaining sex to my son.

IF I KNEW I WAS GOING TO HAVE THREE BOYS,
I WOULD HAVE PAID MORE ATTENTION IN PE

A Flat Sandwich

Bennett, age 10
Kieran, age 9
Ronan, age 7

I read *French Women Never Get Fat* by Mireille Guiliano at the same time I read *How to Feed a Teenage Boy* by Georgia Orcutt.

These books did seem at first to have entirely different philosophies. In her book, Mireille recommended bread, champagne, chocolate, and romance as key ingredients to a balanced diet and lifestyle. She cited her favorite pastimes as breakfast, lunch, and dinner. I thought this would be an interesting read, and it did not disappoint.

Author Georgia was the mother of two tall and hungry teenage boys and the author of many cookbooks. As the mother of three boys who I knew would soon be consuming scary quantities of food, I thought this would be an interesting read, and it did not disappoint.

Mireille started drinking champagne and wine (or at least tasting it) before she was ten. Neither wine nor champagne appeared in Georgia's index at all. Mireille extolled the virtues of small portions of food, consumed with enjoyment. Georgia spoke frankly about how many calories your teenage athlete would need to eat daily. I can tell you this did not mean small portions.

Georgia's book contained a recipe for a sandwich that called for two teenage boys to sit on it for at least 20 minutes before it is eaten. This was called a Railroad Sandwich, which to me evoked packing your lunch on a train in France. But I don't think the French in general, and Mireille in particular, would embrace sitting on something you were going to eat.

Believe it or not, though, these books did have a few important things in common. They both had recipes that emphasized fresh foods, simply prepared. Both books advised staying far away from processed foods and synthetic ingredients. Both authors emphasized the importance of eating three hearty meals a day. However, Mireille claimed French women never snacked, and Georgia said teenage boys definitely have to snack.

I made several of the recipes in both books, but by far the biggest hit from either book was the Railroad Sandwich. I cut the large sandwich in thirds, so each boy could have his own to sit on. It was quite flat at the end of 20 minutes. Those 20 minutes were peaceful, too. Kieran was thirsty and couldn't even bring himself to get up and get a drink of water. Ronan thought it was SO FUNNY that he passed gas while sitting on his sandwich, until a few minutes later, when he got very concerned that it might affect the taste of his dinner. It turned out OK. I did not taste it. And you can be damn sure that Mireille would not have tasted it either.

Tough Question 1

Bennett, age 10
Kieran, age 9
Ronan, age 7

I had one of those tough questions from Ronan.

"Mom, why do only women wear makeup?"

Hmm, so many ways to answer. As with all tough questions, I wondered, what was he really asking?

Luckily, as often happened when I paused long enough after a question, he answered it himself. "Oh, I know, it is to make girls look better. But mom, you don't need it to look better. Most people don't look better. Mom, you look good anyway. Pretty good!"

I gave him a big kiss and told him he was exactly right!

I love that kid.

The Clarinet Has Arrived

Bennett, age 10
Kieran, age 9
Ronan, age 7

A friend brought over her clarinet. She hadn't played in a long time, so she loaned it to us. Bennett was going to start music class at school.

His goal was to get good enough on the clarinet to move to playing the saxophone. The music teacher at school had recommended playing the flute or clarinet before trying the sax. The saxophone seemed to have a considerable appeal to my boys. Somehow, they inherently knew that many people find dudes who play the saxophone incredibly cool.

Bennett was excited about having an instrument to play. His brothers all had to try it out. It sounded like we had a group of very excitable migrating geese trapped inside our house. Maybe the neighbors wouldn't figure out that the mysterious sounds were actually the beginning of what I was sure would be many strange, loud noises wafting from our house. At least, we didn't have a drum set. Yet.

Tough Question 2

Bennett, age 10
Kieran, age 9
Ronan, age 7

Ronan asked me, "Mom, where did Justin Timberlake go to college?"

As with all tough questions, I wondered what was actually being asked here.

Mr. Timberlake did not attend or graduate from college. There was no way I was going to tell my son this. No. I took the opportunity to use my full creative right as a mother and made up my own Public Service Announcement on the benefits of going to college.

I told Ronan that I did not know where Justin went to college. But, of course, he went to college. Yes, I told him, Justin Timberlake went to a four-year university and studied music. His music study involved many instruments and kinds of music and, by the way, a lot of math too.

I was sure he would figure out some day that not all successful people go to college. But he wasn't going to be hearing that from me, at least not when he's in second grade.

IF I KNEW I WAS GOING TO HAVE THREE BOYS,
I WOULD HAVE PAID MORE ATTENTION IN PE

Skimming

Bennett, age 10
Kieran, age 9
Ronan, age 7

My sons spent the weekend studying Newton's Laws of Physics, some cultural anthropology and a new language.

They did this all by competing in the Skimbash in Santa Cruz, California.

The Skimbash was a skim boarding competition at the beach. A skimboard is a flat surfboard-like device used to ride along the beach and in shallow water. The overwhelming majority of skim boarders are boys and men, who have a certain kind of athletic grace combined with fearlessness. It is a small but quite distinct subculture.

What sport could be more attractive to my kids? It was at the beach, and most of the participants were boys, most of them close to their ages, who were incredibly athletic and daring and cool.

There were not many moms there. Thank God, my kids had not realized how uncool it was to have your mom with you at a competition. I had a chance to study these skim boarders, especially the older boys, closely. There were definitely worse crowds to hang out with. The thing that really stood out to me is that skimmers as a group seemed to appreciate creativity, individuality, and innovation.

I have to say, the Skimbash was one of the most unorganized, organized sporting events I had ever been to. But if I was going to be at a competition where no one has the least idea when they might be competing, we might as well be at a beach all day on a beautiful weekend. It was so much better than being at a soccer tournament in a remote rural town on a day when it was 105 degrees in the shade, and I didn't know I had to bring the shade with me.

So, I sat on the beach in my chair and tried to locate my inner zen and let my boys just hang out and skim. I tried to block out the occasionally inappropriate music and concentrated on what words and phrases like dank, rootbeer-style, sex-change, shove-it, schwag and shwack, nar-nar, minibucket, and wrap-it-like-a-Christmas-present could mean. My boys quickly acquired the new language. Too bad I didn't understand a word of it. I could have used a translator.

My husband could not locate his inner zen. Everything about the competition drove him berserk, especially the lack of schedule and having no idea what was going on. He couldn't take it, he had to leave. I had to take it, I'm the one who promised the boys they could compete, and I wasn't about to leave them there by themselves. Too much Red Bull around. Besides, they had been practicing skimming all summer for the competition.

My boys spent most of their waking hours propelling themselves or objects through space. Skimming was a great example of this, with the added complexity of reading the beach slope and ocean conditions and waves. It also required understanding of Newton's laws of physics.

I should have remembered the law, to every action there is an equal and opposite reaction, when I thought I was a cool mom and did some skimming with my boys. I was looking pretty good until I fell. Hard. And the equal and opposite reaction to my wrist was a fracture and the first cast of my life. I'm retired now.

Ronan placed second in his 8-and-Under division, Kieran placed fourth and Bennett placed third in the 9-to-11 division. They each got a trophy, a little carved wooden skimboard.

After School Activity

Bennett, age 10
Kieran, age 9
Ronan, age 7

In the fall, the oak tree near our front door produced an enormous number of acorns, which littered the ground for hundreds of feet around it.

Those tough, hard little acorns really impeded skateboarding, and even walking.

After school one day, Kieran found a hammer in the garage, and the next thing I knew, all three boys were sitting there happily smashing acorns with hammers. It kept them occupied for hours.

Sometimes I just don't get boys.

Ouch My Foot Hurts

Bennett, age 10
Kieran, age 9
Ronan, age 7

I shaved Kieran's leg a few times. Who would have thought that a nine-year-old's legs are so hairy!

I took Kieran to the orthopedist because he said, "Mom, my foot really REALLY hurts." This kid had a very high tolerance for pain, so I immediately made him an appointment. His foot had been hurting for a month or so, and soccer season was just about to start. I started to worry and imagined this very active kid in a cast. It freaked me out. I was more nervous for the appointment than he was.

The doctor carefully examined his foot, manipulated all the bones, and moved it in all directions "Does this hurt?" and "What about this, does this hurt?" He told me, "Your son has Sever's Syndrome. Have him take ibuprofen for ten days and use gel inserts in his shoes. It will go away in a few months."

Huh? What is Sever's? He wrote it down for me and told me, "Look it up on the internet there's lots of information there call me if you have any questions thanks for coming. NEXT!"

Sever's Syndrome is not that exciting for an orthopedist, but I'd never heard of it. I soon learned that Sever's is fairly common.

According to my research, Sever's syndrome is a painful heel condition that affects growing adolescents between the ages of nine and fourteen. Fortunately, it is not serious and is usually temporary.

As the bones of the leg begin to grow longer, they sometimes grow at a faster pace than the Achilles tendon. The Achilles tendon is then too short. It begins to put tension on the back of the heel. When this happens in kids who are active in running and jumping sports, pain occurs where the Achilles tendon attaches to the heel.

A doctor may prescribe anti-inflammatory medicine to help reduce pain and swelling. A small lift or pad placed under the sore heel may help, too. In severe cases, when other forms of treatment don't give relief, doctors may recommend a walking cast for six to twelve weeks. The goal is to stop the foot from moving so that inflammation and pain go away.

I went over this information with Kieran, and he felt better knowing the cause of his pain. When we got to the part about the walking cast, he eyes widened, and he was ready to do whatever he needed to do to prevent a cast. So was I.

First, we went and got him a really good-fitting pair of supportive running shoes. He happened to be fitted by a man who specializes in fitting runners, and people with Achilles issues. He spent a lot of time with us, trying many pairs of shoes until we found one that fit his foot. Then he took the insole out of the shoe and cut some cardboard to fit in the heel area. He put the insole back on top of the cardboard, and had Kieran try the shoe with the gel inserts. After all this, when the sticker shock for this pair of shoes was starting to make me sweat, he gave me a nice discount. I had all three boys with me, and he was sure he'd be seeing us again.

The measures the doctor prescribed helped. And taping up his Achilles for the soccer games really helped too. My husband taped ankles for various sports when he was in college, so he was the Designated Taper (DT) in our house.

The first time we taped Kieran's ankles, he thought it worked great, but taking the tape off was not great. He described it as "ripping my flesh off."

Before we taped it for the next game, we all decided that shaving his leg was a good idea. I, being the most experienced at shaving legs, was now the Designated Leg Shaver (DLS) in the house.

Re-merchandising the Refrigerator

Bennett, age 10
Kieran, age 9
Ronan, age 7

The male members of my family suffered from a disease I call Refrigerator Blindness. It is a disease that made them unable to see what is right in front of them, especially if they are looking in a refrigerator. It caused nonsensical statements like "Mom there is nothing to eat," or "Where is the milk?"

The disease does not affect vision related to desserts, which they could see right through the freezer door. To overcome this disease, I tried to re-merchandise my refrigerator. I was inspired by the beautiful displays at my local gourmet grocery store.

My efforts seemed to be working. I moved the fruit out of the bottom drawer and put it in an attractive bowl, right at eye level. Occasionally, I even paired cheese sticks or slices right in there with the apples. I put healthy snacks like the yogurt and a few hardboiled eggs right at eye level. Cut up veggies went in a clear ziplock or glass dish next to a container of dip. The PB & J were right on the door in easy reach. I packaged up leftovers on a plate if possible, with plastic wrap over it, so it was highly visible. Another technique I learned is to not crowd the shelves too much. Overstimulation caused by a proliferation of food packages and choices made the blindness worse.

Was I crazy to spend extra time art-directing the inside of my refrigerator? I don't know, maybe. But if my boys, and my husband, could look in there and actually see something healthy that they could serve themselves, it was worth it.

Creatures of Comfort

Bennett, age 10
Kieran, age 9
Ronan, age 7

Kieran had a teddy bear that he has slept with since he was a newborn baby. After nine years, Teddy had a somewhat ragged, fragile look to him. I wondered, how long will he sleep with sweet, well-loved Teddy? I knew I would be sad the day Teddy got tossed out of his bed, no longer necessary in the nighttime ritual.

Teddy used to travel with us. But once, when Kieran was four years old, Teddy traveled in a suitcase that lost its way and did not end up in the same airport we did. Of course, Teddy was in a black suitcase that looked exactly like every other black suitcase. We filed a report with the airline and hoped for the best.

Kieran was heartbroken that Teddy was lost. At his urging, I called the airline several times a day. I finally reached a kind soul who went into the Land of Lost Luggage, and starting opening black suitcases until she came to one with a well-worn teddy bear squished inside. Oh, the relief! We were so thankful and relieved to get him back home.

If I Knew I Was Going to Have Three Boys, I Would Have Paid More Attention in PE

I got rid of that black suitcase. I wrote a letter to the airline employee who went out of her way for a little boy (and enclosed a picture of him with Teddy). And we instituted a new rule: Teddy never rides in suitcases.

Bennett also had a Creature of Comfort: a blankie. Blankie was very worn and well-loved, really more of a shredded piece of fabric than a Blankie. Bennett got irritated when Blankie was in the laundry, and to be honest, I tried not to wash it because I was afraid it would disintegrate.

Ronan had Teddy-Bunny and a few other nighttime friends. They rotated in and out of favor, without much attachment to one in particular, so they were not nearly as worn. They didn't get much time in the bed, usually falling to the floor.

My husband had a Teddy bear when he was little. His mother kept it in a plastic bag and gave it to us, years ago, when our children were toddlers. At the time, I thought it was a little odd that she kept this bear. Now I understand.

Seperation

Bennett, age 10
Kieran, age 9
Ronan, age 7

I was going on a trip with some girlfriends, and we were leaving our children behind, in the care of our husbands, all of whom were perfectly capable of running things while we're gone.

Why is it so damn hard for moms to leave their children, even for a vacation that they really want to go on?

The first time I left Bennett after he was born was to go out to dinner with my husband. I had a difficult childbirth and a rough couple of weeks with my new baby. I distinctly remember my mother telling me that I needed some time with just my husband. WHO? I didn't need time with HIM!

She said, "I know, you might not need time with him right now, but he needs time with you."

So, we made plans to go to dinner, somewhere very close by, and my mom babysat. Walking out that door and leaving my baby for the first time was one of the hardest things I've ever done. All rational and logical thought left me, and raw emotion (or was it hormones?) took over. I had to sit in the car for fifteen minutes, sobbing in the driveway, before we could drive away. I couldn't enjoy my meal or think of anything to talk about besides the baby, no matter how hard I tried. I was very anxious to get back home.

With practice, I got a lot better at being separated from my children. It was never easy for me until they were a little older and more independent. But I did it, for my marriage, and for myself, and my kids too. A little space can do wonders for gaining perspective, and recharging.

For me, one of the hard things about leaving children was the organizing. Carpool, sports equipment, lunches, snacks, what they eat for dinner, can my husband do the laundry, will he do the laundry, will the homework get done, bedtime? All this focus on detail distracted me from the thought, the fear, what if something happens to me? What if I die in a plane crash? They still need me! This fear is very real, if somewhat irrational, for most mothers, whether they care to admit it or not. We are hard-wired to care for our children, to nurture and protect them for as long as we can.

But separation was OK, even good. My children gained a little independence, and they even missed me. I, in turn, got some time away, a chance for a unique adventure or to learn a new skill, gained some perspective on daily life and my parenting. I might even get a glimpse of the possibilities in store for me when my children really don't need me so much anymore.

I needed practice for that too.

Note to Live By

Bennett, age 10
Kieran, age 9
Ronan, age 7

Why it is not a good idea to pee on people because they may have to take a shower. Also they may not like it and they will go screaming around. The person who did it may think it is funny while the other person goes and tells on you.

"You may go into your room," Mom said.

That is the reason to not pee on somebody!

The end.

> *—written as a reflection per my request, after incident between brothers, identity withheld.*

Why I Hate Halloween

Bennett, age 10
Kieran, age 9
Ronan, age 7

I hated Halloween because it produced situations like this: twenty pounds of candy in the house, 537 pieces to be exact, collected by one very proud Kieran.

All this candy caused:

Eating candy like a half-starved animal, by him, and sometimes by me.

Sugar-induced mood swings.

Ownership and sharing confrontations.

Breakfast, lunch, snacks, and dinner required candy desserts.

ENOUGH! It must go!

The five of us had a one-and-a-half hour intensive negotiation session.

Final settlement:

Four-piece allotment on weekend days, two-piece allotment on weekdays, for ten days. The overachieving candy collector got a bonus of ten pieces. The remaining candy was to be donated to a charity of collector's choice. He chose "construction workers who can burn it off without getting fat." This of course was not a real charity, but rather than argue that point, my husband swept it all into a big bag and promised to deliver it to construction workers. After taking a large commission for his office, of course.

Free Time

Bennett, age 10
Kieran, age 9
Ronan, age 7

I could just barely hear what sounded like a play-by-play, somewhere in the house. Bennett and Kieran were supposed to be getting ready for bed.

I went in and checked on them and, unexpectedly, on the laptop screen, there was a gigantic eye. They were both riveted by a cow eye dissection. Kieran had a dissection coming up in science, and he wanted to see what it would be like.

I am convinced that these are the kind of moments that happen when you have a little free time. Time to explore an interest or to play. We were a busy family, and one of the few ways I could figure out to carve a little more free time was to severely limit television consumption in our house.

My boys rarely watched TV growing up. It was really not such a foreign concept for me, I rarely watched TV growing up either. Without it, we had a little more time for lingering over dinner, reading stories, and playing outside. Occasionally, the boys even (gasp) got bored, and had to figure out how to entertain themselves. We did watch a few things

If I Knew I Was Going to Have Three Boys, I Would Have Paid More Attention in PE

every once in a while; cooking shows, sports, and the news if there was a big world event. We watched a movie occasionally. But it wasn't a regular thing we use to fill up time.

Like me, the boys will most likely grow up to be absolutely terrible Trivial Pursuit players. They, too, will feel the frustration of not being able to contribute to small talk centered around the latest television shows.

But really, it was a small price to pay for all those little moments of inspired playtime. And cow eye dissections.

Mad Mad Minutes

Bennett, age 10
Kieran, age 9
Ronan, age 7

The Mad Minutes drove me mad. They drove Ronan mad too. And my husband. We were all mad for Mad Minutes. Mad Minutes revealed one of those touchy subjects of parenting: the inevitable comparison.

I tried not to do it. I really tried.

Comparison is a natural, if not always wise, way for parents to gauge how their child is doing. Is my child better or worse? Ahead or behind? More athletic or more musical? More talented or harder working? Artistic or a shit-disturber? Comparison among siblings is a way to gauge strengths and weaknesses. And among siblings, there are certainly different strengths and weaknesses, as living within a family can make so plainly clear.

We tried our best to recognize that each child was different, and had their own special qualities, different styles of learning, and different interests. We honored the person our child was right at the moment. Most of the time, this worked pretty well.

But how was Ronan so different from his brothers? What was going on here?

Ronan had just started Mad Minutes in school, a sheet of math facts to be completed in a fairly short, timed period. He started out with simple addition. In the years to follow, it would progress to multiplication and division. The object of the Mad Minutes was to master or memorize the math facts, so they could be done correctly and quickly.

Bennett and Kieran sailed through Mad Minutes. They rarely studied for them, maybe a few practice sheets here and there, and they would pass each level and move to the next. Not Ronan. He had been stuck on the same sheet for a month.

Ronan's brain doesn't work the same way his brothers' do. He needed a lot more practice, a lot more repetition. It was much harder for him to concentrate and focus on accuracy and speed. I reluctantly got out the flash cards, thinking maybe they would help. They were still brand new. The flash cards frustrated both of us. I tried explaining a few rules and tricks for memorizing the addition facts, and I think that just confused him. We were annoyed with each other, and he was still stuck on the same page.

My husband came to the rescue. He happens to be very gifted with numbers. He approached the issue with more patience and more concentrated time, and figured out how to help Ronan. He observed what wasn't working and found a method that did. He became the official Mad Minutes parent. Apparently, I couldn't do it.

"Wow," my husband said to me after one long study session, "his brain works a lot more like yours."

Compared to his brothers, Ronan was way behind on his Mad Minutes. Compared to me, however, he was doing just fine!

So, I guess if we are going to compare our kids to others, it matters who we compare them to.

And Your Point Is?

Bennett, age 10
Kieran, age 9
Ronan, age 7

Bennett announced, "Mom, guess what! I am going to be the point guard on the basketball team!"

Football just ended. I think I was starting to sort of follow it. And with no adjustment time at all, I was thrust into another sport that I didn't understand.

It's a little embarrassing to admit that I didn't really get basketball. I mean, I knew the basic basics. I knew that players needed to be tall, and I knew who Steve Nash was. But considering how many college basketball games I had been to in the last 15 years with my husband, who comes from a family of rabid college basketball fans, I really should have known more than that.

So, was a point guard the player who guards the other team from getting a basket?

Is it going to matter that my son is the most, eh, height-challenged player on the team?

The Short Life

Bennett, age 10
Kieran, age 9
Ronan, age 7

At dinner one night, Ronan announced quite seriously that he is only going to live to the age of eleven.

He said it in a slightly sad, matter of fact way.

"Why?" I asked curiously, with a touch of concern.

He gazed levelly at me as if I really should know the answer. "Global warming."

Hmm. This kid was much more worried about the destruction of our environment than he was about the terrorist threats that were all over the news. I wondered if the current president would take a phone call from a seven-year-old who would like to realign his priorities.

IF I KNEW I WAS GOING TO HAVE THREE BOYS,
I WOULD HAVE PAID MORE ATTENTION IN PE

Coffee Helps

Bennett, age 10
Kieran, age 9
Ronan, age 7

I was having a hard time adjusting to the daylight savings/lack of daylight savings, whichever it is, time change.

Actually, it was not the time change that got to me. Not that I didn't enjoy having the same argument-discussion with my husband — and then my boys — every year. Were we springing ahead or falling back, would we have more sleep or less sleep, more daylight or less, and what time was it really?

WHATEVER!

It didn't make much sense to me. What made a lot more sense is to wake up when it is light outside, and go to bed and read by candlelight when it gets dark.

I wanted to throw my clocks out the window and live by my own circadian rhythms. Less daylight, plus less outside time for kids, equaled a grumpy Mom.

A Day Off from Parenting

Bennett, age 10
Kieran, age 9
Ronan, age 7

I spent my Saturday at traffic school. It was advertised as Pizza and Comedy Traffic School. I expected the instructor to be the comedian, but it turns out the students were.

As we went around the room sharing how we got our tickets, I got more and more nervous because my story was so stupid and boring compared to the others.

There was the straight-haired college student sitting next to me, doing crosswords, reading Harry Potter, and drinking a can of guava juice. She told us she got a ticket speeding because she was listening to a terrible song, and also wore her seatbelt under her arm.

There was Mr. Proud Prius Driver who got a ticket for speeding even though he was under the impression cops never gave tickets to Prius drivers.

There was the blonde 50-year-old woman with a big smile, who said she was enjoying life and listening to a good song, in her daughter's car, cruising down Highway 5 doing about 100 mph (160.93 km/h). When she was pulled over by, in her words, a really HOT cop, she whipped out a picture of her brother in his police uniform and asked if that would help her. It did, and she was written up for a slower speed, and qualified for traffic school.

There was the 16-year-old boy who just got his license and got a ticket for speeding but insisted he didn't deserve the ticket, even though he was speeding.

There was Vladimir, a tall man in dark glasses, dark slacks and dark turtleneck, with an accent so thick, none of us could understand what his ticket was for. The instructor told us that before the class, Vladimir parked and re-parked his shiny black car in the parking lot three times in three different spaces, so stay away from it. Vladimir's cell phone went off five times during the class, each time blaring Russian ballet music that the instructor told him to get rid of.

There was Chris, who was very drowsy and trying to get some shut-eye. When it was his time to share, he mumbled something about getting a ticket on his motorcycle. He looked hung over in a bad way. Then I thought, oh, maybe he's stoned. Yeah, he was stoned.

Then, my favorite fellow student, Monty, introduced himself. He was about twenty and recently got his license. He told us he rode his bike to traffic school. He got his ticket because he was driving extremely recklessly and ran two cars off the road. One of them was a cop. Lucky for him, it turned out the cop was an acquaintance from high school, so he got off with traffic school instead of jail.

What did I learn at traffic school?

Don't eat tacos while driving. They are the number one kind of food eaten by people when they get in an accident.

I learned that, lacking any other tools, you can put an injured deer out of its misery with a skateboard. This was from Monty.

I learned that there is actually a law against transporting anyone in your trunk.

I made a mental note. When my boys start driving, warn them not to eat tacos in the car.

A Song vs. A Poem

Bennett, age 10
Kieran, age 9
Ronan, age 7

A good friend turned me on to Billy Collins reading his poetry.

My boys and I became Billy Collins fans. We listened to him in the car when I wanted a change from bickering or Top Ten. My favorite poem of his is *The Lanyard*, about a mother and son.

Occasionally, we listened to Monty Python in the car. That is, until I heard Ronan singing "Every Sperm is Sacred" to himself. I think I would rather have him quoting poetry.

Bad Dinner Party Behavior

Bennett, age 10
Kieran, age 9
Ronan, age 7

It was very rare, with three young boys, for our whole family to be invited to a dinner party. So of course we accepted the invitation. The hostess had a son the same age as one of mine. There were two other families with their children included as well.

With nine kids in total, the hostess wisely hired a neighbor to watch over the kids, serve them dinner, and keep an eye on them. The kids had a table to themselves, ate dinner early, and then went to another room, away from the adults, to play. Meanwhile, the adults had a lovely dinner at the large dining table decorated with fresh flowers, and set with crystal wine glasses.

Conversation centered around the sub-prime mortgage collapse, as each couple had some connection or was affected in some way.
Despite sounding dreary, it was lively, sometimes veering off to other topics such as schools, and Van Halen concerts.

Shortly after we began to eat, the oldest of the children present in the other room, a 13-year-old

IF I KNEW I WAS GOING TO HAVE THREE BOYS, I WOULD HAVE PAID MORE ATTENTION IN PE

girl, came in and whispered in her mother's ear, then crouched nearby playing a hand-held video game. The mother mentioned to no one in particular that there was some bad behavior going on among the kids. I assumed she was referring to her child, or one of the boys I didn't know. Of course, she was not talking about MY children.

She left the table to check on the kids, came back, sat down heavily, filled up her wine glass, and stared at me. Wait, did I miss something? Why does this woman look like she wants to slap me? I narrowed my eyes.

She leaned forward in a sort of conspiratorial, malicious way, and said across the table, "I want to tell you that Ronan was beating up my daughter and he is really not a nice kid. I'm telling you this because if MY son did anything like this, I would want to know about it. Is this the way he usually acts?"

What do you do when someone insults your child in the middle of polite dinner conversation? I mean, besides calling them a bitch? I just sat there and stared at her, incredulous. I really liked the friends who hosted the party, and I did not want to ruin the dinner. I'm not a confrontational person.

So, wondering what my little second-grader could have possibly done to this eighth-grader, I told the woman that I would investigate. But I would do it later. Then, I turned to another guest at the table, and joined another conversation.

A few minutes later, I caught my husband's eye. Engaged in another conversation, he hadn't heard what the woman said to me. He immediately said, "What's wrong?" I had that look that spouses instantly recognize in each other, the "I'm really pissed off" look. He started to panic, thinking I was angry with him, when I motioned to the woman next to him. He rolled his eyes, letting me know he understood and sympathized.

As soon as we were in the car on the way home, I instituted an absolute dictatorship. I announced I would hear what went on from Ronan, with no interruptions or comments from anyone, and then Bennett and Kieran would have their turns.

I was seething mad, but knew I didn't have the whole story. It turns out that the eighth-grader had refused to share a video game or let Ronan have a turn. And she picked on him, told him girls were better than boys, that he was a bad person, and repeated told him to shut up.

Ronan admitted his anger got the best of him, but he insisted he did not hit her. He was hitting the back of her chair. Kieran backed up his story, and Bennett said it was such a minor thing that he

If I Knew I Was Going to Have Three Boys, I Would Have Paid More Attention in PE

didn't even notice anything was going on. The babysitter didn't notice anything amiss either. Kieran said that when the mother came to check on the kids, she was particularly rude to Ronan. All the kids noticed that.

How to explain all this to Ronan, who was hurt and confused? My god, I couldn't even explain it to myself.

My husband came to the rescue.

Utterly uninformed of the situation until we got in the car, he summed it all up for the boys. He told them that 13-year-old girls are creatures to be wary of. They can be unpredictable and not very nice. Be careful and steer clear of them.

I guess that goes for their mothers too.

I'm not confident it was the best explanation. But I had to agree with it. I was a 13-year-old girl once myself. Thank god I have boys.

Birthday Suit

Bennett, age 10
Kieran, age 9
Ronan, age 7

Bennett's eleventh birthday was coming up.

He was a minimalist, not interested in collecting things, or acquiring possessions.

When I asked him what he wanted for his birthday, he was surprisingly specific.

He wanted a suit. From Dad. Not from Mom.

"Because," he said, "a suit is Dad's department."

I didn't know where he would be wearing his suit. Out to breakfast on Saturday morning? To a meeting with his teacher about the next book report? To baseball try-outs?

I was not sure how to interpret this, but I have to admit it made me sad. He was growing up.

IF I KNEW I WAS GOING TO HAVE THREE BOYS,
I WOULD HAVE PAID MORE ATTENTION IN PE

Santa's What?

Bennett, age 11
Kieran, age 9
Ronan, age 7

I knew I lived in a house with boys when the phrase "Santa and his sack" met with such giggly laughter.

Every single time.

I had never thought of Santa as an anatomically correct man before. Kinda grossed me out.

Just Go With It

Bennett, age 11
Kieran, age 9
Ronan, age 7

Ronan announced, "I know Santa is really moms and dads. But I'm just going to go with it."

I was saddened by the fact that my youngest child no longer believed in Santa, but impressed with his honest and matter-of-fact way of letting us know.

Bennett and Kieran had never challenged the Santa Myth so directly. There had been comments about the impossibility of Santa's gift-giving journey around the world in one night, or how exactly he could fit down the chimney, and what about houses that don't have chimneys? What about the kids who don't get any presents from Santa because they're Jewish?

I answered all these questions, which cannot be answered, by saying something similar to "It's magical, isn't it?" I tried my best not to directly lie.

Now we had to have the rather difficult conversation about preserving the beliefs of younger friends and especially younger cousins. How to explain that he needed to perpetrate the myth? I really didn't want

If I Knew I Was Going to Have Three Boys,
I Would Have Paid More Attention in PE

my sisters mad at me for destroying Santa at
their houses. I'd rather leave that up to their friends
at school.

While mourning the loss of innocence in my house,
I didn't notice that Ronan had not only turned into a
skeptic, he was now a snoop. Every second in which
he was not being directly watched, he was
rummaging around through closets and rifling
through drawers, looking for Christmas gifts.

I was unprepared. For years, I could leave an
unwrapped gift lying around in almost plain
sight and no one would notice it. This year, Ronan
probably discovered every present before I'd had
a chance to wrap it. He might have known
exactly what he was getting, and he might have
known exactly what his brothers were getting
for Christmas.

I believed in Santa for a long time, until I was
probably ten years old. I thought only Santa could
possibly know how much I wanted my very own
giant jar of sweet pickles, and another year how
much I wanted that massive set of plastic Barbie
shoes and purses in every color.

Some of my friends told me that the youngest child
tended to be the one who questioned the status quo.
This was a desirable trait in an adult, but not in a
seven-year-old who was out of school, hyped up on

See's Candies and beside himself with excitement a couple of days before Christmas. I had to take him to my husband's office for a couple of hours so I could wrap and hide things. And so I could hear myself think.

I thought that the next year I may be forced to take the advice of a wise friend, who told me that he arranged to drop off all the gifts for his three children at a friend's house. He provided all the supplies, and the friend wrapped everything and held on to the gifts until they were ready to put them under the tree.

This was a revolutionary idea to me, something I just never would have come up with myself. It's genius really.

IF I KNEW I WAS GOING TO HAVE THREE BOYS,
I WOULD HAVE PAID MORE ATTENTION IN PE

Jesus Christ!

Bennett, age 11
Kieran, age 9
Ronan, age 7

I am a fan of musicals. When I had the opportunity to buy tickets to Jesus Christ Superstar, I envisioned a great family experience, sharing my love of the music with my sons. I looked forward to the performance for a long time, and as it got closer, played the soundtrack, so the boys would be familiar with it.

Showtime! I eagerly led everyone to the third row center seats. Right up in front! The best place for kids to sit for a musical, I thought, right where they are almost a part of the action.

Wrong. Really wrong.

It was right when the noose lowered down from the ceiling, and Judas was singing his guts out about his torment in betraying Jesus, that I realize what a big mistake I made in bringing my boys. I saw Jesus Christ Superstar once before, but obviously didn't realize it would be so, well, really so inappropriate for a seven and nine-year-old.

Don't get me wrong, the music and most of the singing was fantastic.

But seeing a man playing Judas, sticking his head into a noose on stage mere feet away from our third row seats, was not good. The actor was black, which made this scene even more uncomfortable. I tried to block Ronan's eyes. It shouldn't have been hard, as he was sitting on my lap and had been since the second song. He fought me off, but didn't want to get back in his seat.

Things continued on very intensely to the ultimate scene. Yes, Jesus nailed to the cross. Mere feet away, we bore witness to a 60-year-old man, playing Jesus, nearly naked, nailed to a massive cross, moaning, groaning, gasping, panting, struggling, calling for his mother, and truly suffering for what seemed to be at least 15 minutes. It was taking him forever to die.

Ronan was absolutely transfixed by the scene, and my legs were going numb with the weight of him on my lap for two hours. I couldn't even begin to explain to him what was going on, so I kept whispering into his ear, "Just concentrate on the music and the singing. Just listen to the music." Kieran was two seats away from me, I couldn't talk to him at all.

If I Knew I Was Going to Have Three Boys, I Would Have Paid More Attention in PE

What was I thinking? My boys were too young for the graphic, violent, dark and complex story line. What if they ask me about Mary Magdalene? Was this really the best way to introduce them to the story of the life of Jesus? You couldn't get a more different impression than the gentle hippy man wearing a dress and petting a lamb, that other kids learn about in Sunday school. This Jesus was scary, even to me. Especially so close up.

At the end of the show, leaving our row, Kieran asked if he could check out the guitar player he caught a glimpse of in the orchestra pit. Glad for the diversion, we all looked at the musicians, keyboards, electric guitars, and computers that produced the wonderful music for the show. Walking out into the chilly afternoon, I contemplated all the questions that were going to be asked of me in the following days. I was pretty sure none of them would be about the music.

Knitting on New Years

Bennett, age 11
Kieran, age 9
Ronan, age 7

Nicole, a friend of mine, came to town for a brief visit. She is, among other things, an experienced knitter and an art teacher.

Nicole was helping me to accept the fact that my knitting project, a whole sweater I had worked on for quite some time, was a failure. It needed to be un-knit. Yes, completely unraveled; the body, both sleeves, everything. No way to save it. My gauge was way off, and it was huge, too huge for anyone in my family. After tearing up, I mourned the loss for a while, and she counseled me about getting "back on the horse" and working on a project I could be more successful at. Like a small washcloth.

Watching all this drama, Ronan hung around fondling all the yarn. He asked, "Can I try?"

Nicole didn't hesitate. "Sure!" She has taught many kids to knit. She was patient and encouraging and soon had him happily knitting away, making a washcloth.

IF I KNEW I WAS GOING TO HAVE THREE BOYS,
I WOULD HAVE PAID MORE ATTENTION IN PE

I'm sure she didn't realize what she started. Now all three boys wanted to knit, and I didn't have enough yarn. So, we headed to the craft store. We went to the craft store because I felt it would be better not to take them to the beautiful yarn store, with exotic and expensive choices. It would have been too overwhelming for them and me.

We headed straight for the yarn isle. It took about 15 minutes of fondling and caressing and discussion to pick out yarn. They were magnetically attracted to the most expensive, softest yarn the store stocks. We negotiated and settled on some choices. Then we picked out the needles, a different color and size for each boy. A few customers paused to watch us, but the boys saw nothing unusual about getting knitting supplies; they were excited.

Once home, we rolled the yarn into balls. Then we got started. I sat with each boy and gave him a few instructions. The lesson was really basic, since I am a beginning knitter as well. They started knitting away.

I marveled at the sight for a moment and then spent the next several hours trying my best to answer questions, checking work, fixing dropped stitches, helping to unravel mistakes, and generally being the constant on-call knitting doctor. I couldn't get anything else done.

This was a problem as it was New Year's Eve, and I had not yet shopped for dinner. My husband surveyed the scene when he arrived home from work, perplexed and amused. He learned to knit as a boy as well. He started cooking the only thing he knows how to cook; macaroni and cheese. We ate quickly. Everyone wanted to get back to knitting.

Ronan wondered aloud who invented knitting. I consulted my knitting book and read to them that no one really knows who invented it, but that traditionally women produced the yarn, while men did the knitting. This did not seem odd to them, of course men did the knitting. Because it is really fun and cool.

This was perhaps the most bizarre New Year's Eve I have ever experienced. No entertaining, no champagne, no count-down, no resolutions, no elaborate goodbye to the year ending and a new one beginning.

Instead, we stayed up late, knitting the old year into the new one.

IF I KNEW I WAS GOING TO HAVE THREE BOYS,
I WOULD HAVE PAID MORE ATTENTION IN PE

More Yarn

Bennett, age 11
Kieran, age 9
Ronan, age 7

We needed more yarn.

What, oh what, have I done?

I had three sons obsessed with knitting. They were even immersed in the language, discussing dropped stitches, increases, and decreases (all unintentional), and purling. They accused one another of making their stitches too tight. Wise observations were made; if you have bigger needles, you can get more done.

We were already out of yarn. Was the craft store open on New Year's Day? We drove over with much anticipation. YES! It was open and we were the only customers. We got more yarn. Projects could progress.

Kieran spent the day alternating between knitting, reading his Alex Rider book, and singing along with the Jesus Christ Superstar soundtrack.

Lacy Lichen, Stinky Chiton

Bennett, age 11
Kieran, age 9
Ronan, age 7

The boys and I visited Point Lobos State Reserve during winter break, one day before a big storm swept in, and we would be homebound for a few days. It was our first visit to this small but achingly beautiful and dramatic point of land just south of Carmel, California.

Point Lobos is small enough to hike around in a day or two, but the variety and drama of the landscapes and vistas around every corner make even the most active, rock-climbing, exploring boy pause in wonder. It was the kind of day that inspired poetry.

Lace Lichen

Lace lichen

hanging from trees

like woven cotton

in the winter breeze

sits lace lichen.

I've always dreamed of it.

>   *—by Ronan, composed in situ, on the trail at*
>   *Point Lobos*

If I Knew I Was Going to Have Three Boys,
I Would Have Paid More Attention in PE

Lacy Lichen, Stinky Chiton

I am made to explore

jellyfish and whale bones as big as park benches,

divers just coming in or just going out

dripping

seawater and equipment.

Trails through ghostly trees,

lacy lichen waving to us

it needs only the fog to live,

while we need a hearty

picnic lunch and a peanut butter cookie.

The barking of distant sea lions arguing

a point of land rising straight

above a churning misty sea

rocks like sheaves of paper stuck in the shore.

Trees covered in soft carrot-colored

moss misnamed green algae.

A sign, pointing to a secret which is no longer hidden,

a cove full of pebbles and caves, abalone shells.

A large chiton, unmoored, waiting to be discovered.

A large rock, tall in the center of the beach, waiting to be summited.

Two sweatshirts each and we are shivering,

misty air loosing light

minivan cozy and warm,

windburned cheeks turn hot.
A day of . . .
what
is that smell
quick
find a bathroom
with a sink and some soap
don't touch a thing
not the seatbelt
not the door
not me
that chiton you were holding
I think it had an odor!
    –*by me, composed after our visit to Point Lobos*

If I Knew I Was Going to Have Three Boys,
I Would Have Paid More Attention in PE

It's Alarming

Bennett, age 11
Kieran, age 9
Ronan, age 7

After winter break, we all had to rely on our alarm clocks to get out of bed for the school day. It was cloudy, it was cold, it was dark, it was Monday. Hit the snooze and roll back over.

Each boy had an alarm clock, which had several options for alarms, including various nature noises, which no one used.

Bennett set his on the classic alarm beep. Why? He said it was simple, and it woke him up. It didn't make him want to go back to sleep like music, and didn't freak him out like the sounds of the rainforest.

Kieran had his alarm clock set to sports-talk radio. Why? Well, of course, you could never get enough sports!

Ronan had his alarm set to play music, the local top 40 station. Why? Because he loved music. And a good song or a bad song could determine how his morning went.

My husband set his alarm but never heard it because he always woke up before the alarm, and turned it off. Why? I didn't know, and it was a little spooky.

I set my alarm to news-talk radio and slowly rose into consciousness with the sounds of familiar voices telling me about traffic accidents and slow-downs on various freeways. I listened to the weather forecast. Every so often, I hit the snooze. Then I usually got at least one boy hug, from someone coming in to check on me and make sure I was awake.

It used to be that I woke up first, and then made sure my boys were awake. I was their alarm clock.

But since I was not so much a morning person, and each person liked to wake up in their own way, it really was much better to have all the alarm clocks. It made for an interesting cacophony in the hallway. Alarm clocks were never grumpy, even on Mondays.

IF I KNEW I WAS GOING TO HAVE THREE BOYS,
I WOULD HAVE PAID MORE ATTENTION IN PE

Why Nine is Great

Bennett, age 11
Kieran, age 9
Ronan, age 7

Nine years old. What a great age to be. Not too big, not too little, but just right.

Your Nine-Year-Old: Thoughtful and Mysterious, by Louise Bates Ames, describes Nine as a tricky age; unpredictable, independent, persistent, complaining, moody, and hovering on the brink of adolescence.

Ooo, it's that last part, that adolescence part, that I could see now in Kieran. In my opinion, that was precisely the reason to celebrate the inconsistencies of the age. Kieran had not discovered eye-rolling and the snarky comments that Bennett was beginning to master. He was in the sweet spot, between a little boy and an adolescent.

The independent and persistent part of being nine was on display at Little League baseball try-outs. He approached the try-outs with confidence and anticipation. He caught every pop fly, threw accurately and hard, hit a home run, and threw his pitches right into the catcher's glove.

Yet, this confident and capable baseball player was still a little boy. That night, when he went to bed, he couldn't find Teddy. Teddy has slept with him every night since he was a baby. When Teddy was unaccounted for, the whole house went into high alert, as we all knew how important he was. Kieran had to find Teddy, and couldn't possibly sleep without him.

I knew it was fleeting, that he would cross into adolescence soon. I was just going to enjoy the age he was at nine, and the look of simple joy on his face for the two of the things he loved, baseball and Teddy.

IF I KNEW I WAS GOING TO HAVE THREE BOYS,
I WOULD HAVE PAID MORE ATTENTION IN PE

The Harry Potter Effect I

Bennett, age 11
Kieran, age 9
Ronan, age 7

How do I know if my son is completely obsessed with a Harry Potter book?

Kieran was missing at carpool pickup after school. After a lengthy and increasingly frustrating search all over the campus, he was found sometime later in the bathroom . . . reading.

Bad Birds

Bennett, age 11
Kieran, age 9
Ronan, age 7

There was a hawthorn tree near our kitchen window. In the winter, it was bare of leaves, but full of bright red little berries. One day, two different flocks of birds invaded the tree, hopping around and eating all the berries. It was fun to watch.

Suddenly, we heard a BOOM! BOOM! BOOM! The boys and I and jumped up to find three little delicate birds on the ground outside our glass front door. Two were panting but otherwise completely still, and the third was clearly dead, head at an unnatural angle, wing splayed, a bit of blood. There was much interest and concern from the boys, observing the birds from such a close range. I had to do a bit of convincing to keep them from trying to pick them up.

There was some speculation that the berries the birds had been eating had intoxicated them and impaired their judgement and flying ability.

"Yes, these birds ate the berries and then stupidly flew right into the glass, and now they are hurt and one is dead," I said, grasping at the opportunity. I took advantage, whenever I could, to reinforce the negative effects of drugs and alcohol.

Ronan carefully studied the still birds for a bit longer, then looked up at the tree, birds still swarming around the berries, unaware of their fallen friends.

"Mom, are those gangster birds?"

Light it Up

Bennett, age 11
Kieran, age 9
Ronan, age 7

I went to a parent education night at my boys' school and came away with this nugget:

> A mom's most important job is to make sure her face lights up when she greets her child. A dad's most important job is to love his children's mother. And his next most important job is to remember that she is not HIS mother.

It doesn't solve all the world's problems, but this reminded me to make sure I gave each of my boys one heck of a big, genuine smile and hug at least once a day.

This was not as easy as it sounds, when they were talking back to me and rolling their eyes and constantly grabbing my cell phone to change the ringtone.

If I Knew I Was Going to Have Three Boys,
I Would Have Paid More Attention in PE

First Signs of Spring

Bennett, age 11
Kieran, age 9
Ronan, age 7

Spring was on the way. I could tell.

Not by the weather warming up *(it wasn't)*.

Not by the flower buds appearing *(not yet)*.

Not by the bees buzzing around *(too cold still)*.

Not by the butterflies fluttering through the yard *(didn't see any)*.

No, it was the lovely sound of a baseball hitting the side of the house,

THUNK!

that announced spring was coming.

It wasn't real close, but was coming.

The Harry Potter Effect II

Bennett, age 11
Kieran, age 9
Ronan, age 7

Kieran had still been reading Harry Potter obsessively. In the car. While eating breakfast. While doing homework. While he was supposed to be sleeping. He was closing in on the final chapters of the fifth book, exclaiming it was the best book so far.

He came home from school the other day and told me he had a problem. While Bennett and Ronan tell me this kind of thing all the time, it is rare coming from Kieran. I sat down and gave him my full attention.

"You know Andy at school?"

Yes, I knew Andy. He was the football coach, and a physically imposing disciplinarian at the school. He was a stern and not exactly chatty person. I was a little scared of him myself.

Thoughts raced through my mind. What kind of problem could my son have with Andy?

IF I KNEW I WAS GOING TO HAVE THREE BOYS, I WOULD HAVE PAID MORE ATTENTION IN PE

"This is a big problem."

My heart started pounding.

"Andy has the next TWO Harry Potter books checked out from the library."

The First Valentine's Day That Really Matters

Bennett, age 11
Kieran, age 9
Ronan, age 7

Bennett's first Valentine.

He had friends who are girls, but this was different.

She was not the little girl he liked to hold hands with in pre-school. She was not the little girl with waist-long hair, who in kindergarten could make him happy with her radiant smile.

No, this was a girl he really liked, and who liked him back. A girl he asked, via email, to be his Valentine. A girl who said yes, of course she would be his Valentine and signed her email "love u." A girl he actually talked to on the phone (for about 40 seconds).

He wrote a note to her. "For some reason I was thinking about Valentine's Day! You are so going to be my Valentine. You're an awesome friend. Could we be boyfriend/girlfriend super secretly? Please!"

Gulp. This was the real thing. A real crush.

He said he wanted to give her something more than "just a card" to on Valentine's Day. He asked me for some suggestions. We pondered flowers (too embarrassing to bring to school), something sweet (chocolates, homemade cookies). Thank goodness, the conversation did not veer off into jewelry. I left him to decide on his own. I could tell this was something that needed to come from his heart.

Considering that he would need to go through some elaborate measures to make sure he could secretly deliver his Valentine presents to school, he decided on a special cupcake, and a DVD of the movie Shrek 3. He spent almost all the money he had, earned by doing yard work, on the gifts.

Seeing evidence of a romantic side in my son was a really touching experience. How innocent and thoughtful he was. For the first time in our house, Valentine's Day was not all about candy and the chore of making cards for all their classmates.

It was about that thrill of a first crush reciprocated.

Ever watchful, Kieran and Ronan observed it all with a shrewd eye. What did they think of this special Valentine? Interestingly, they didn't tease their brother. Ronan rolled his eyes. Kieran commented, "I think giving her Shrek 3 is kind of weird. I'm glad I don't have anyone to give a special present to."

I said to him, "Maybe next year."

And he replied, "Yes, probably next year."

IF I KNEW I WAS GOING TO HAVE THREE BOYS,
I WOULD HAVE PAID MORE ATTENTION IN PE

The Harry Potter Effect III

Bennett, age 11
Kieran, age 9
Ronan, age 7

Newsflash! Kieran finished the last Harry Potter book. He proclaimed it the best one in the series, and said he wished it went on and on and on. He hoped JK Rowling will come out with a new series. He was excited and dejected at the same time to have finished.

It's hard to believe this is the kid who didn't like to read until about the middle of third grade last year.

To all you parents of boys who struggle with reading, patience!

Now, if only I could take my own advice. Ronan was in second grade and not a fan of reading at all.

Three Boys and a Funeral

Bennett, age 11
Kieran, age 9
Ronan, age 7

It was a sad day when our first pet died.

It was not technically the first loss of a pet in our family. We had a cat who ran away. But there is a big difference between a pet running away, with its uncertainty and lack of closure, and a pet dying.

Our pet rat, Summer, officially belonged to Kieran, but all the boys enjoyed playing with her and taking care of her. She swelled up, stopped eating or pooping, and couldn't move very well. She was listless, and Kieran became alarmed. So did I.

I was alarmed because I thought she was going to die. My boys were alarmed because they thought she was pregnant.

I told them she couldn't be, there was no boy rat around. They had some crazy immaculate conception theory which I flat out rejected without much explanation. The topic here was death, not some kind of miracle.

If I Knew I Was Going to Have Three Boys, I Would Have Paid More Attention in PE

I called a few different vets in my town, only to be told they don't see rodents. Rodent? She's not a common rodent! Oh, I guess she is.

I didn't know what to do. Taking a rat to the vet might seem absurd, but the poor thing was clearly suffering. So, I called my mom. I had pet rats when I was young, and I asked her if we had ever brought any of them to the vet.

She said, "Well, maybe once, I'm not sure. Your rats didn't get sick, they just died." She offered to call her vet, in a more rural town about an hour away. Sure enough, they saw all types of animals there and she got me an appointment. And then because she sensed this might be difficult, she went with me to the appointment.

We stood outside the building looking at the two front doors, one labeled "Cats" and one labeled "Dogs." We had a little debate as I carried Summer in her cage across the parking lot. Which door?

We went in the Dog side and much to my relief there was a room between the two which was either a quarantine area or neutral territory. It probably should have been labeled "Not Cat or Dog." We sat together and waited for Summer's name to be called.

Once Summer was gently examined by the very kind vet, I was asked if there were any boy rats around. Geesh, did I have to defend her virginity again?

Then we discussed the three options. Exploratory surgery. *No.* Aspirating the fluid in her abdomen and seeing if it comes back, which the vet told me was certain *No.* Or end her suffering and euthanize her. I decided the most humane thing to do would be to end her suffering.

As I said goodbye to Summer, I got choked up and started crying. It was much harder than I thought. The vet asked if she should leave and give me a few minutes. "No," I choked out, "it's okay." Tears streaming down my face, I held Summer, stroked her, and said goodbye.

The vet said, "She's been a good rat." My mom whipped her camera out of her purse and took a few photos.

I asked to have Summer's body, so I could bring it home and the boys could say goodbye to her. An important part of having a pet is learning about death, so I brought Summer home in a little cardboard box. The boys knew there was a possibility that Summer would have to be put to sleep, and they were sad when I told them that evening.

If I Knew I Was Going to Have Three Boys, I Would Have Paid More Attention in PE

Bennett, to cover up his sadness, smirked uncomfortably, and pragmatically informed us that rats don't live very long. Kieran wanted to know what was wrong with her, why she got sick, and how the vet put her to sleep. As I told them the story and the three options the vet gave me, Ronan said, "So the three choices were death, death or death?"

The funeral was held on Saturday after baseball practice. I prepared the boys, letting them know exactly what was going to happen and how it was fine to feel sad and cry if they wanted to, but also fine if they didn't feel like crying.

All five of us proceeded to a spot my husband decided would be a good place, under a huge old oak tree, for the burial and funeral. Kieran and my husband dug the hole. We opened the box and looked at Summer, lying peacefully on her side, and the boys said goodbye. Tears welled.

We got out the eulogy the boys wrote, and Kieran started to read it. His voice cracked, he choked up, and had to pass it to Ronan to continue reading. Struggling, Ronan handed it over to Bennett, who by now had huge tears rolling down his face. My husband and I added a few kind words, and placed the box in the hole. The boys filled in the hole with dirt, and made a marker with sticks and a few flowers. Walking back to the house, Ronan was sad, and we cried together while I reassured him that it was normal and okay to feel sad.

"What," he asked, "are we going to do with her cage?" A little later the boys were curious to know exactly what would happen to Summer's body in the ground, and it was my cue to remind them of the cycle of life, and how her body would turn back into dirt eventually.

Death is such a difficult concept to discuss, especially with children who have different levels of understanding about it. But we had some good practice, thanks to Summer, who was a good rat.

Goodbye, Summer the Rat

You were

Funny

Very playful

Willing to move her cage

Very explorative

She had fun anywhere

Very affectionate

When I was sad she helped me feel better

Very happy

She would like to come out of her cage when we opened it

She was very snuggly like going in the hood of our sweatshirt.

The end.

> *—eulogy written by Bennett, Kieran and Ronan*

Almost immediately, the sadness moved to discussion about who would like what pet next. I told them I preferred not to discuss that for a few days.

I needed some time. This was harder for me than it was for them.

Hanging with the Girls in Gold Country

Bennett, age 11
Kieran, age 9
Ronan, age 7

Fourth graders in California study California history, so what better place to go than the site of the discovery of gold in 1849? My sons went to a school that participated in an Outdoor Discovery School overnight field trip. I was thrilled to make the cut as a chaperone.

For some of the fourth graders, this was their first trip away from home and parents, and excitement was running high as we waited to leave. I must admit, my nerves were a little on edge. You see, I was not going to spend three days with my 4th grade son Kieran. I was going to chaperone seven 4th grade girls. Of course Kieran would be there, but he would be chaperoned by a dad, who had one child, a girl. Now that I think about it, he might have been more nervous than I was, or at least he should have been.

I was nervous because as ridiculous as it may sound, I was no longer used to girls. I mean, I grew up one of three girls, and I am a girl, but I was not around them very much. I felt like I was out of touch with the girls. At the least, I thought, I would have a lot to observe about the differences between boys and girls.

It turned out there were a few differences, but not as many as I expected. The girls in my group cried a bit more than the boys. There was a crazy kind of contagious teary homesickness thing that started late in the evening on the first night. One of my girls got sad and started crying at the square-dancing hoe down. As I was comforting her, another girl in my group noticed the tears and started crying. Although this girl was nearly as tall as me, I had her sit on my lap. Then, another girl noticed what was going on and didn't want to be left out and started to cry as well. Luckily, a teacher noticed the contagious emotional outburst and came to help out. All was soon calm. The teacher checked to make sure I was okay, and I told her if I started crying, then there was a problem.

I discovered that some girls snore just as loud (or louder) than boys. Their clothing was everywhere in the cabin. They couldn't find their socks. They didn't want to shower or comb their hair. They woke up in the morning and immediately began discussing what was for breakfast, exactly like Kieran would do.

I really enjoyed being one of the girls, instead of the only girl, for a few days.

I've Got Baseball All Over My Calendar

Bennett, age 11
Kieran, age 9
Ronan, age 7

The schedules came out, and I put all the Little League games and practices, for all my boys, on my calendar. It took me hours, and it was all color coded. It looked like an Excel spreadsheet threw up on my calendar.

There was only one day a week when we didn't have a game or practice. Every day after school we would be choking down a quick snack and searching for all the various baseball uniform items; pants, socks, belts, undershirts, jerseys, hats, sliding shorts, hat, and cleats. And the required athletic cup, the hardest item to find because it traveled all over the house, I had no idea how.

All items were constantly in various stages of being clean or dirty. At the beginning of the season, we sprayed all the grass stains with stain-remover, attempting to have the boys look clean. We usually gave this up by the third week or so, and they wore the pants in whatever state they were in; clean or dirty, stained or not.

If I Knew I Was Going to Have Three Boys, I Would Have Paid More Attention in PE

After long practices and even longer games, which could last two and a half hours, there was little time for homework, preparing and eating dinner, showering and reading and bedtime. No playdates, no television. My friends and family knew that I was always out at the baseball field or driving to or from, and never called my home phone during Little League season.

And yet, call me crazy, it was fun.

Rhymes with Fiancé

Bennett, age 11
Kieran, age 9
Ronan, age 7

Dogs were a big topic of conversation around our house. We explored getting a dog, and discussed other dogs we knew.

I overheard Ronan explain to a friend how his aunt and uncle just got a puppy, a male dachshund named Vinny, and his nana and grandpa have a little female dachshund named Rosie.

Someday, he told the friend, the dogs are going to get married and mate.

"But right now, they are just Beyoncé."

IF I KNEW I WAS GOING TO HAVE THREE BOYS,
I WOULD HAVE PAID MORE ATTENTION IN PE

Well, It's About Time

Bennett, age 11
Kieran, age 9
Ronan, age 7

I made an important discovery: athletic tape is to boys what bandaids are to toddlers.

A sore thumb, a hurt ankle, a wrist sore from writing, it could all be made to feel much better with athletic tape. And just like those Spider-Man bandaids when they were younger, the tape seems to have some sort of attention-getting fashion appeal too.

My husband helped pay his way through college by taping ankles and other assorted body parts for various college sports teams. You would think this would be a big help when it comes to taping up scrawny little preteen wrists. But no, he is not home when all this taping needs to occur. Thank god for the internet and the wealth of information on how to properly tape up just about any body part. With a roll of tape by the front door and one in the car, I was ready for anything.

Riding in the car on the way to baseball practice, Ronan whined about how his wrist hurt from taking a fall. So, I offered to tape up his wrist before practice if he would like.

He replied, "Wow, you are a REAL boy-mom now!"

Tough Question 3

Bennett, age 11
Kieran, age 9
Ronan, age 7

Kieran asked me, over dinner at a nice restaurant, "Mom, were you the hottest girl in your class?"

I never did figure out a satisfying answer to that one.

Baseball Took Over My Life

Bennett, age 11
Kieran, age 9
Ronan, age 7

Between feeding, outfitting and transporting my three Little League baseball players, I had scarce time to do much else during the season.

I really enjoyed the games, though. Thank goodness or I would have gone crazy. All my non-Little League friends wondered what happened to me. I disappeared for months. Between practices and games, I was at the field from four to six days a week.

If I was lucky, I remembered what day I was snack mom and who has grown out of their cleats and where I last saw that athletic cup lying around the house. Where is that team jersey in the laundry cycle? When did I have snack shack duty, and did I update the latest practice schedule changes from the 87 emails a week I got related to Little League?

To avoid eating out all the time, I often started planning and preparing for dinner right after school started in the morning. I tried my best to provide healthy and filling after-school snacks, which were often as big as a dinner. Trying to provide dinner

IF I KNEW I WAS GOING TO HAVE THREE BOYS, I WOULD HAVE PAID MORE ATTENTION IN PE

within five minutes of getting home from practice and games after being gone all afternoon was really challenging and took high-level organizational skills.

If my children did not truly love baseball, there is no way in hell I would have put myself through this. Kieran loved baseball so much that he proclaimed he wanted to be a professional baseball player when he grew up.

I wondered why when the trophies were awarded at the end of the season, I didn't get one. My husband had several trophies as a coach. I figured if I got a trophy for assisting each boy through each baseball season, and another for each All-Star team, I would have ten trophies lined up on my nightstand so far, and I would be eagerly awaiting more.

Sports, Illustrated

Bennett, age 11
Kieran, age 9
Ronan, age 7

I'd thought about taking a class in sports photography, since I felt like I was going to be doing it for the rest of my life.

No soft-focus romantic shots of little girls with flowing hair, holding flowers in the dappled sunlight, for me. I wanted grit and determination on a contorted face, the ball frozen in space, image stabilizing, a macro lens, a photograph so detailed you could almost smell the sweat.

I wondered, did I need to really understand the game to take great sports pictures?

I shocked myself by passing up the *People Magazine* and picking up a *Sports Illustrated* in the doctor's office waiting room. I studied the photos in it.

I was starting to wonder what was wrong with me.

IF I KNEW I WAS GOING TO HAVE THREE BOYS,
I WOULD HAVE PAID MORE ATTENTION IN PE

Little League Etiquette

Bennett, age 11
Kieran, age 9
Ronan, age 7

Why the heck did people, friends and strangers alike, congratulate the parents of a child who hits a home run? There was excitement and high-fives all around. But we were not the ones who hit the ball. The etiquette around this perplexed me.

How was a parent supposed to act? Proud, but not too proud? How are we supposed to walk the fine line?

No one liked a bragger, especially the Little League dad with his "My kid beat up your honor student" bumper sticker.

What were we supposed to do about the Proud Grandma? The one who believed she earned the right to sit in the stands and loudly cheer praises of her grandson, while at the same time trash-talked all the other children and the volunteer umpires out on the field.

Note: This Proud Grandma was not related.

Mother's Day

Bennett, age 11
Kieran, age 9
Ronan, age 8

Mother's Day fell during Little League season. In honor of baseball moms, I share this quotation. It's just a reminder of how seriously people take the game.

> If I were playing third base and my mother were rounding third with the run that was going to beat us, I'd trip her. Oh, I'd pick her up and brush her off and say, 'Sorry, Mom,' but nobody beats me.
>
> *—Leo Ernest "The Lip" Durocher, Brooklyn Dodgers, Manager*

IF I KNEW I WAS GOING TO HAVE THREE BOYS,
I WOULD HAVE PAID MORE ATTENTION IN PE

Exposed

Bennett, age 11
Kieran, age 9
Ronan, age 8

I itched uncontrollably upon receiving an email from my boys' school. An exposure notification. Not chicken pox this time. Not strep throat.

"Your child has been exposed to lice. It is highly contagious. Please check your child every day for the next two weeks and immediately report any cases to the school office."

I immediately went to the drugstore to see what tools I could find to check my boys every day for two weeks. My children weren't even home from school, but I wanted to be prepared.

I wandered through the shampoo and hairbrush section and didn't find what I was looking for. Lice detection and treatment was not where other hair-related products were sold. That would be too logical.

It was in the aisle with the fungicides, jock itch sprays, athletes' foot medication, wart removers, and pinworm medication. I have purchased each of these items in the past. I hate this aisle of the drugstore. It is the gross isle. I never had to enter this aisle until I had three boys.

When we needed the pinworm medication, I couldn't even go to the store. I sent my husband. He gamely went and got it. In a different city.

I thought I was done with the gross aisle for a while. But no, the lice stuff is right there too. I bought the metal lice comb and drove home.

Since my children were not home from school yet, I started to obsessively comb my hair with the lice tool, searching for evidence.

I questioned my children after school and although it's supposed to be confidential, all three of them quickly named exactly who had been sent home with lice. There was no hope of anonymity in this situation. Then they told me that even a teacher had been sent home.

I found no lice on myself or any of my boys. They all enjoyed the combing, which was a little weird. I made my husband submit to the combing, and he didn't dare argue about it. I felt like a mother gorilla grooming her family.

Well, except for the part where they eat the bugs they find.

If I Knew I Was Going to Have Three Boys, I Would Have Paid More Attention in PE

I did discover while combing my hair with the lice comb that I had dandruff. That must be why I was itchy! I had to head back to the drugstore.

At least dandruff shampoo was not in the gross aisle.

All Night Party

Bennett, age 11
Kieran, age 9
Ronan, age 8

We went to Family Camp in the mountains over Memorial Weekend.

Boys: Camping is SO FUN! You get to sleep in a sleeping bag in a tent.

My husband and me: Camping is a pain in the ass!

Putting up a large tent by the light of the car headlights and a single flashlight held by a wildly excited eight-year-old Ronan was a test in patience. We uttered curses under our breath at the tent, and each other, as we tried to appear to the other cheerful campers who arrived much earlier, like we were already having fun.

Boys: This tent is so COOL! It's huge!
Us: This tent is big!

As soon as we moved five sleeping bags, all our clothes, pillows, and shoes in, it was completely full. This thin nylon house was neither warm nor did it muffle any sound. We could hear the bullfrogs, dropping leaves, the footsteps and conversations of other campers walking by, and they could hear our children belching.

Boys: I slept great but I was a little cold.
Us: Sleep?

I was so cold that even though I had to pee pretty bad sometime in the middle of the night, I didn't even consider getting out of my sleeping bag. Sometime later, my husband and I were awoken (if we were asleep) by a crunching of sticks and leaves by some large heavy feet, just outside our tent. Pause. Silence. Then slurping and licking noises.

"Honey, there is a bear."

"I know. It's out there and we're in here. I'm not going out there to chase it away."

Slurp, slurp.

"It's really close."

I tried my best to stay very still and fall asleep, even though there was a bear nearby, separated only by a thin piece of nylon. I was freezing cold, and I really really had to pee. Then just before dawn, we heard the gentle tapping of a light rain on our tent. By morning, I was exhausted.

Boys (shouting): Look at the lake! Is it breakfast time? What's for breakfast? Can we go out in a boat? Can we go fishing? Can we play basketball?

Me: Where are my shoes? They better not be wet.

The boys peed outside the tent. I trudged up to the bathrooms and noted that it was at least 20 degrees warmer inside the unheated bathroom than it was in my tent.

Boys: See ya!

Us: Hey isn't this *Family* Camp?

Yes, but we understood we would hardly see our children again until it was time to go home. They quickly joined up with friends and disappeared for hours at a time. We would spot them maybe during meal times.

It started to heavily mist, and then sprinkle. My husband climbed back into his sleeping bag and didn't emerge for several hours. I headed to the craft shack, where I gamely tried to sit and summon my creativity. My hands were soon too cold to be functional.

I wandered back to the tent to check on my husband, who opened one eye and said, "Just give me the word and we can be packed up and out of here in an hour."

If I Knew I Was Going to Have Three Boys, I Would Have Paid More Attention in PE

Ronan discovered the joys of the walkie-talkies I brought. There was no cell phone coverage at camp, but I was paged every five minutes by my son who was less than a hundred feet away and wanted me to know that he found a really cool stick.

In the dining hall, I heard that a bear broke into a bear-box in the night and ate all the food out of it, including a watermelon. Ah ha! The slurping all of a sudden made sense.

After lunch, my husband and I decided to go on a walk around the lake to warm up. It was a two-mile walk. Ronan was in a boat on the lake fishing. I called him every five minutes on the walkie-talkie to tell him where we were and that I found a really cool rock.

The kids were pretty warm during the day because when they woke up, they just put on all their clothes over their footed fleece pajamas.

The sprinkles turn into a steady cold rain. Someone said, "It's almost snowing!"

We came to the realization that we shouldn't sleep in the tent that night. We wanted to avoid being cold AND wet. We sent Bennett and Kieran to sleep with other families who were intelligent enough to book cabins rather than a tent site. We asked around and were very kindly offered a place to sleep in a friend's cabin. They evicted their own two children to sleep in other family's cabins, so there was room for us.

I found out in the morning that Kieran stayed up playing cards until 1:30 am. My husband went to take down our tent, which was indeed very wet and soggy. He came back to the mess hall, with freezing hands, for breakfast. We had to leave the mess hall, though, because the group had to eat in two shifts.

Luckily, there was a room nearby called the library where we were to wait for our shift. While it sounded great, the library turned out to be a nursery room with fake wood panelling, a short table and tiny chairs, and a mesh climbing structure in the middle. Once this small room filled with hungry, cold adults and children, it was very similar to being in Chuck E Cheese. My husband disappeared. I found him packing the car.

We gave the kids the news: after dinner and square-dancing, we are heading home. The boys were absolutely indignant. How could we make them leave early?

For some reason, our children thought that going to Family Camp was by far the best trip they could ever go on. I didn't get it, but after some extensive questioning, I think I figured out why they liked Camp so much.

If I Knew I Was Going to Have Three Boys, I Would Have Paid More Attention in PE

They liked the freedom of running around with friends, and they liked the sense of community. They knew nearly every person at the camp and have known many of the families since they were in preschool. They liked all the traditions of camp (most of which were cancelled due to weather), the s'mores, the campfire songs and skits, the fishing, hiking, swimming, popsicle stick boat races, pajama breakfast, and the conga line dancing to "All Night Party."

This year, it was a little too much like roughing it and not enough like relaxing. Each year we wavered about going back to Family Camp. If we go next year, we are ditching that stupid tent and staying in a cabin.

On our drive home in the middle of the night, through 38 degree weather, fog, rain and hail, the boys slept and my husband and I talked and I read to him as he drove. It was warm and dry in the car, there was no traffic, and it was by far the most relaxing part of the trip.

A Momentous Week

Bennett, age 11
Kieran, age 10
Ronan, age 8

Kieran experienced a momentous week. He had his tenth birthday (double digits!), hit a game-clinching home run in a playoff game, and was given unexpected news by the ophthalmologist: he no longer needs to wear glasses!

He could not imagine a better week.

It was pretty good for me too.

I was told by a random stranger that I looked far too young to have a ten-year-old. I watched the look of sheer joy on Kieran's face as he rounded the bases after that home run. I watched the coach from the other team have a tantrum.

Most significantly, I was freed after five long years from keeping track of eyeglasses that needed adjustment on a weekly basis and seemed magnetically attracted to the car bumper and basketballs in the face.

IF I KNEW I WAS GOING TO HAVE THREE BOYS,
I WOULD HAVE PAID MORE ATTENTION IN PE

Playoffs Play On

Bennett, age 11
Kieran, age 10
Ronan, age 8

No matter how exciting it was to see my son's Little League team win a game in the playoffs, it meant yet another game. And therefore, another disruption and reshuffling of our schedules.

Playoffs came right at the end of the school year, which was a crazily busy time. Between the three grades and the various teams the boys were on, almost every night we were going to some sort of end-of-year or end-of-season event. Each of us went way over our yearly quota of greasy pizza, limp hot dogs and overcooked cheeseburgers. The baseball pants were no longer white and had holes. The batting gloves were torn to shreds. The hats had distinctive sweat rings.

I was driving a minivan around, emblazoned with my son's team names. Every time I took a corner, baseballs rolled and thumped from one side of the van to the other. There was more than one athletic cup under the seats. The cleats, caked with dirt, were getting too small. I had to go to the grocery store at least once, and sometimes twice a day. I blamed it on my complete lack of ability to plan anything. I never knew if there was going to be another game or if the team was finished!

I watched each playoff game with such mixed emotions. The result might mean several afternoons free, or another game and team snack duty. It would determine if we could count on dinner and time to do homework the next evening, or if we would be at the field again until 9:00pm.

Playoff games did not tend to bring out the best in the parents or the coaches. In some cases, it was quite the opposite. Come on, people, let's not act like the outcome of this one game would send us to the Little League World Series. Now THAT was a terrifying thought.

Soon we would get a phone call, inviting one or maybe two boys to play on All-Star teams, yet another extension of the season. It was an honor, a great experience, of course yes, he would love to. How could we say no?

Baseball Results

Bennett, age 11
Kieran, age 10
Ronan, age 8

Little League went on and on. Ronan's team came in second in the league. Bennett and Kieran's team came in first place in the league, which meant that they then went to the Tournament of Champions. Their team kept winning, including the last championship game. They went as far as they could go. They were really proud of their accomplishment. Kieran, who was the closing pitcher in the final game, was in the local paper.

The peer pressure to decorate my car for the playoffs and All Stars was very strong. I put my own twist on it, so it was universal for the rest of the season and I didn't have to keep changing it. My minivan sported this across the rear window: Little League + 3 Boys = Too Many Balls. I was very amused with myself and enjoyed the occasional honks and thumbs-up while driving around.

The day after their team won the TOC tournament, Bennett and Kieran started practicing with their respective All-Star teams. All-Star practices involved almost three weeks of three different practices a day. One team practiced twice a day, the other once a day, every day. None of these practices were at the same drop off or pick up time or location. And then each All-Star team had four games, at different locations and mostly overlapping times. It felt like I was living inside a word problem on a math test.

What did I learn from all this winning? Boys expect an absolutely enormous trophy, roughly analogous to the World Series Commissioner's Trophy, for winning all the games. Not a little medal they wear around their neck. I also learned that my local carwash took advantage of baseball moms by charging them $12 extra to remove car decorations that came off with water.

While all three boys loved to play, Kieran was truly passionate about baseball. As a 10-year-old, he described his "most spiritual moment" in his life as the day Dad told him he was signed up for Little League. We watched Field of Dreams, and he declared it was the best movie in the entire world. He was happier on the baseball field than anywhere else, according to him.

I started to comprehend the fact that baseball would be a part of his life, and mine, for quite a while.

IF I KNEW I WAS GOING TO HAVE THREE BOYS,
I WOULD HAVE PAID MORE ATTENTION IN PE

Deep Breath

Bennett, age 11
Kieran, age 10
Ronan, age 8

The school year was over, the Little League season finally ended, it was almost August, and summer officially started for me and my family.

I felt like I had had to go on a baseball detox program. So there is no misunderstanding, I did actually enjoy baseball. What I struggled with was the frequency and inflexibility of the practices and games. It took over not just my boys time, but all of my time as well.

For months, I didn't have time for myself. I didn't have the energy to write, although I certainly had plenty of material. I didn't have time to cook healthy meals and spend time at the table with my family. I didn't see my friends or family unless they came to a baseball game. All this and the mandatory duty in the snack shack, where I sold snacks and food, just about put me over the edge. There was not one unprocessed, remotely healthy item offered on the menu.

I recovered, getting in the groove of slower days, which I relished. We ate better. And I became a less stressed and much nicer person.

Was it possible to have three boys playing Little League and not go insane? It must be, I saw other moms doing it. There was one mom I knew that made me feel like I just didn't have my shit together. She had three boys, all playing Little League and competitive soccer at the same time, and she came to every game with a huge supply of snacks. She was on time. Anything her kids (or mine) asked for, she pulled out of her bag. She score-kept for games, was the team mom, organized pizza after the games, volunteered for extra duty in the snack shack, and always looked put together with her nails freshly manicured.

The bitch.

What was her secret?

I had to figure this out before next season.

Acknowledgements

Raising boys takes a village.

Thank you to my entire family, especially my mother, who has enthusiastically encouraged each and every one of my various artistic pursuits.

Tremendous thanks to the teachers at the Mountain School parent co-op where my sons went to preschool. I would not be the parent I am without your guidance.

Thank you to the teachers and others at Hillbrook where my sons attended elementary and middle school. Your encouragement and support of each son's talents was outstanding. "Be kind. Be curious. Take risks. Be your best." Special thanks to Scott, their PE teacher. We all learned so much from you.

Thank you to the teachers, counselors, and coaches of Bellarmine College Preparatory in San Jose California, who challenged and inspired each son, in his own way, to become a man for and with others.

Thank you to my friends, who have supported and walked with me through both successes and disasters. You know who you are.

www.ingramcontent.com/pod-product-compliance
Lightning Source LLC
Chambersburg PA
CBHW020654060526
44119CB00069B/32